HAND TO HAND
COMBAT
FOR
AMPHIBIOUS SCOUTS

The Naval & Military Press Ltd

HAND TO HAND
COMBAT
FOR
AMPHIBIOUS SCOUTS

...

UNITED STATES NAVAL AMPHIBIOUS
TRAINING BASE
FT. PIERCE   FLORIDA

...

C. GULBRANSON, CAPTAIN USN
COMMANDING OFFICER

Published by

The Naval & Military Press Ltd
Unit 5 Riverside, Brambleside
Bellbrook Industrial Estate
Uckfield, East Sussex
TN22 1QQ England

Tel: +44 (0)1825 749494

www.naval-military-press.com
www.nmarchive.com

PREFACE

This manual has been prepared as a guide to the Hand to Hand Combat course taught the Amphibious Scout. The material contained herein, is primarily derived from the combat forms of the Ten Shin Shinyo Ryu system of Jiu Jitsu.

The student who expects to be successful in hand to hand combat must maintain a physically fit body and an alert mind. He must practice until he has gained real speed and precision in the execution of these forms and should review frequently to maintain his skill. Boxing and Jiu Jitsu should not be considered rival systems of fighting. They supplement each other perfectly and the smart student of hand to hand combat will acquire a knowledge of both.

It is to be noted that Jiu Jitsu is more than an unrelated number of bone breaking holds. It is a method of fighting based upon the principles of leverage, timing, momentum, equilibrium, vital touches, and above all, the principle of non-resistance or the taking advantage of the opponent's efforts. The student should practice the tricks both right and left handed with the above principles constantly in mind. When proficiency has been gained he will find that he is able to, in any situation, instinctively devise his own trick, different than those contained in this manual, but based on the same principles and every bit as good.

I wish to express my thanks to Lieut. Colonel Linwood Griffin, USA., for his helpful criticism and for his preparation of the chapter on Knife Fighting.

A. J. HOPKINS,
Lt. Comdr., USNR.

APPROVED:

C. GULBRANSON
Captain, U. S. Navy
Commanding

BRIEF HISTORY OF JIU JITSU

The Japanese trace the origin of Jiu Jitsu back to the Mythological Ages and give various stories to account for it. It is generally credited that during the Ming Dynasty in China, the art was introduced from that country to Japan. There exists in North China today, a system of self defense that seems very closely related to the Jiu Jitsu practiced by the Samurai. It seems quite evident, however, that it's perfected form is due entirely to Japanese efforts.

At the close of the feudal era in Japan, the best known schools scattered throughout the empire were: Shimmei Sakkawatsu Ryu, Ryoishinto Ryu, Arato Ryu, Kyushin Ryu, Kito Ryu, Asayama Ichiden Ryu, Kiraku Ryu, Sekiguchio Ryu, Tenshin Shinyo Ryu, Yoshin Ryu, Takenouchi Ryu. These systems were based upon practically identical principles, though sometimes applied in a different manner. The most highly accredited of these schools was probably the Tenshin Shinyo Ryu. The basic principle or aim of the old schools was to gain control over an armed or an unarmed assailant. This "control" consisted of a very evident threat to life or limb so as to bring about a surrender of the opponent. The control was to be gained, if possible, without injuring the opponent. If necessary, however, he was to be injured or killed to gain the control.

When Admiral Perry opened up Japan and modern civilization and fire arms were introduced the instructors began to lose their pupils and Jiu Jitsu was rapidly becoming a forgotten art.

In 1882, Baron Jigoro Kano originated a new school of Jiu Jitsu that he called Judo or Jiudo. This method was evolved by taking from and modifying other systems and is based upon almost identical principles as certain schools of past ages, Kugusuka, Yawara, Kumuichi and Kempo. It elaborates upon Tia Jutsu which was a part, but far from being the whole, of the older schools of Jiu Jitsu. Jiudo is taught primarily as a sport, and as a method of physical and mental culture. It concentrates on tripping and throwing (Tia Jutsu). The dangerous leverages and blows are not stressed, and are not taught to the student until he has spent a number of years mastering the throws. Jiudo as a sport has become very popular. It has practically displaced all other systems of Jiu Jitsu and has become so well known that the very word Jiudo is now used interchangeably, though mistakenly, with the word Jiu Jitsu.

TABLE OF CONTENTS

TABLE OF CONTENTS

TABLE OF CONTENTS

Caution!

Because of the dangerous nature of Jiu Jitsu all possible precautions must be taken to prevent injury while studying the art.

The submission sign is two quick pats on your own or your partner's body. If both hands are tied up two stamps on the mat.

When a hold becomes painful give the submission sign. Be expecially cautious of elbows, as they will snap without much preliminary pain.

Release a hold immediately when the submission sign is given.

Practice all holds slow motion. Do not become excited and apply a hold with a quick jerk or snap.

Do not resist a hold when it is being practiced on you. Cooperate with your partner so that he may learn the proper technique and do not try to enter into a contest with him.

Speed is developed through the elimination of lost motion by perfecting the technique. It is not developed through trying to do a trick 'fast'.

Falls and Rolls

HAUCHI "HOW TO FALL WITHOUT HURT"

The force of a fall is broken by turning the downward force into a rolling force, and by beating the mat with the stiffened arm and the soles of the feet. Beating tends to rebound the spine before it hits, and prevents the instinctive placing of the hand to catch oneself which could result in a broken wrist. Beating with the flat of the feet helps break the force of the fall but it is usually preferable to cross the legs as an aid in quickly recovering an upright position.

A person skilled in falling can take a hard fall on a concrete sidewalk with no more injury than a stinging of the arms and feet.

TEACHING TIPS

Tell the student to beat six inches from his hips. It is seldom that he will do so and it is satisfactory if the arm beats further out, even up to a ninety degree angle from his body. The effort to beat closer will improve his form.

Insist that the hands are turned in when going into a forward fall. This will help prevent sprained wrists. As the student gains proficiency and takes longer dives he will tend to point his fingers forward. There will be no harm to this now.

Training must be progressive with the student building up to the harder falls. Do not force a man beyond his capabilities or the result will be a sprained shoulder, or even a sprained or broken neck.

When throwing a man release him for an easy fall and hold onto him for a hard fall.

PRELIMINARY EXERCISES

Turn a number of simple forward somersaults keeping the head tucked in and the body rolled up tight.

Lay on the back and bring the hands together about six inches above the stomach with the arms held stiff. Strike the mat with the palm and arms about six inches from the hips as hard as possible. This should be a rebounding blow the arms returning to their former position.

Lay on the right (left) side and roll onto the back beating the mat with the left (right) arm.

Lay on the back twist up onto the left hip. Cross the right leg over the left and stamp with the flat of the right foot outside of the left knee. At the same time beat the mat with the left arm. Alternate to the right and left.

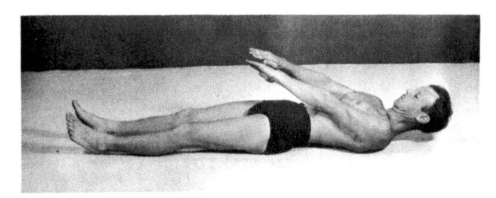

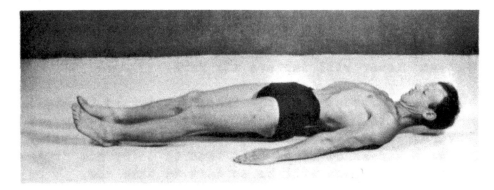

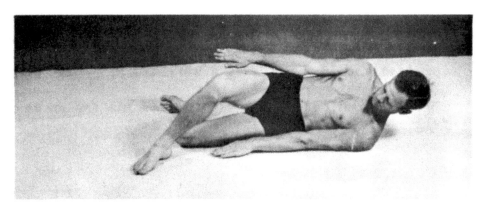

FRONT FALL

Place the hands on the mat with the fingers turned toward each other and touching. Tuck the head in tight, chin pressing against chest. Turn a somersault by springing forward making first contact on the back between the shoulders. Repeat the above arching the back beating with both arms and stamping with the soles of the feet. Repeat springing forward a little further and progressively dive over greater space.

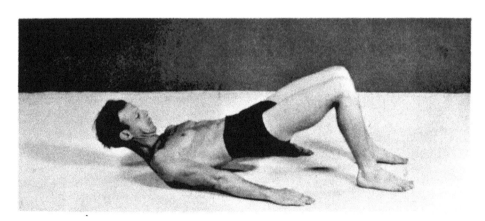

SIDE FALL

Place the right foot forward. Put the right
and left hands close to the inside of the right ankle.
Tuck the head well in, force both hands back and lift
up on the left leg. You will fall into a roll that is
partly straight forward and partly to the right side.
Beat with the left arm and stamp with the flat of both
feet.

Repeat springing forward a little further and
progressively dive over greater space.

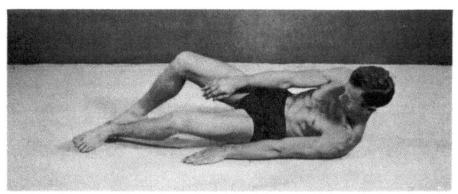

BACK FALL

Sit down, roll onto the back and beat with both arms and stamp with the feet. Arch the back and keep the head tucked in.

Sit on the heels and repeat. Stand up jump back and repeat.

REGAINING A STANDING POSITION

The feet may either be stamped to help break the force of the fall or may be placed in such a position that they aid in recovering an upright position.

As you fall, bend your left leg at the knee so that your left ankle is under the knee of your extended right leg. The force of the fall will roll you up into a standing position. Turn to the left on the balls of your feet as you roll up so that you are facing the person who threw you.

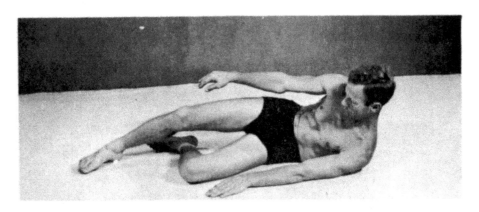

FALLING WITH A RIFLE

Hold the rifle in the "Port Arms" position.
Raise it slightly and tuck it in close to the chest.
By tucking in the head it will now be possible to
make forward and side falls as outlined before. The
beatings with the arms in this case must be dispensed
with.

Hold the rifle in the "Port Arms" position
run forward lean down and extend the arms so as to
drive the butt of the gun into the ground. Fall into a prone position on your stomach breaking the
force of the fall by supporting your weight on the
rifle.

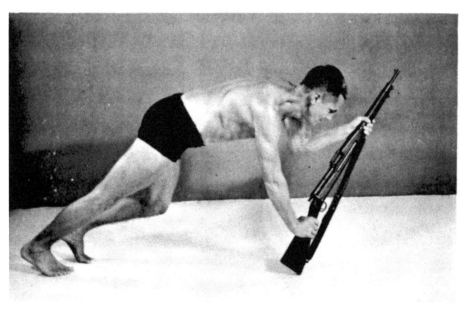

THROW #1, OINAGE "TOSS OVERHEAD"

Kneel on your left knee. Your companion
standing behind you, places his right arm over your
right shoulder. Grasp his right hand with your left
and his right shoulder with your right hand. Pull
down on his arm and lean forward so as to throw him
over your head.

You are standing and your opponent grasps
you from behind, his arms over yours. Lift your arms
so as to loosen his grip and at the same time reach
for his right hand and shoulder, drop to your left
knee and throw him as above.

Master the throw as given above and then
start using the right foot to kick back on the opponents right ankle when making the throw.

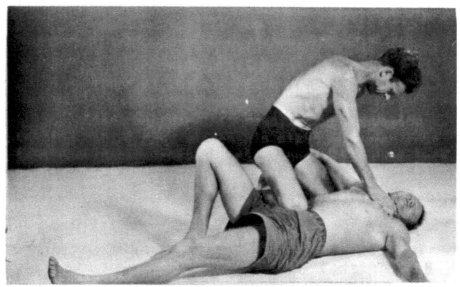

THROW #2, SUKUI "SHOVELING."

Grasp your opponent's right elbow with your
left hand and his left shoulder with your right hand.
As your opponent pushes you or rushes into you plant
your left foot and keeping both legs perfectly stiff
sit down. Keep the legs at a ninety degree angle and
perfectly stiff and allow the right leg to swing outside of and behind him. Pull down on his right elbow
and push up on his left shoulder and throw him over
your left leg.

THROW #3, UDE - MAKIKOMI "ARM TWIST"

From your opponent's right side grasp his
right hand with your right hand and pull his arm
across your chest. Pass your left arm under his right
arm to the back of his neck or grasp his left coat
lapel. Throw yourself onto your back so that your
head is just in front of his feet. With a firm twist-
ing hold on his right hand, force your opponent over
your body to your opposite side.

CAUTION: This is an extremely hard fall.

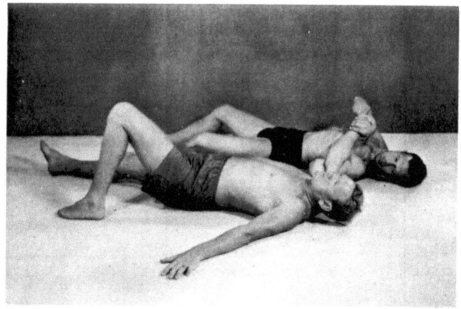

Defense against Weapons

DEFENSE AGAINST WEAPONS

The defense of an unarmed man against one who is armed can be divided into two distinct steps: First the block or diverting the weapon and Second the counter-attack.

The block or diversion requires speed and precision which can only come from continuous practice.

The counter-attack follows the block as rapidly and with as much economy of motion as possible. Usually several different counter-attacks are possible.

Considerable time should be spent practicing the blocks and diversions only. When the counter-attack is practiced, care must be taken that the block is still cleanly done and is not slighted in the eagerness of making the counter-attack.

In the following forms it is assummed the weapon is held in the right hand.

DEFENSE #1

PISTOL HELD IN FRONT

Raise your hands as ordered. Do
not extend them any higher than necessary to
satisfy his demand. The upper arm should be
horizontal, elbow on the same level as the
shoulder. Watch his eyes. When he shifts
his eyes from yours slap down hard against
the knuckles of his gun hand with your open
left hand, diverting the gun to his left.
At the same time pivot your body to the left.
After striking instantly grasp his hand.

COUNTER-ATTACK

You are holding his right hand with
your left. Drive your right hand onto the
back of his hand and twist it back and outward applying Form #1.

Alternate counter-attacks would be
Form #8 or to pull his arm across your chest
and apply the arm leverage described in
Escape #12.

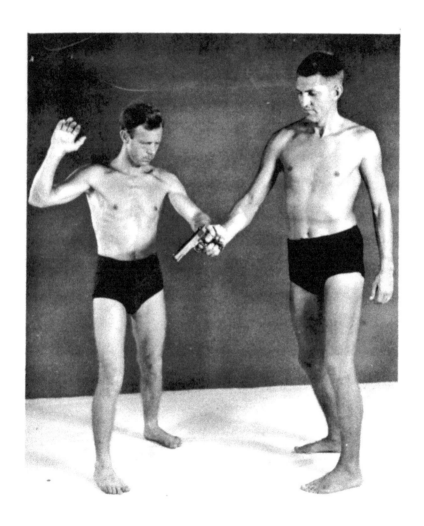

DEFENSE #2

PISTOL HELD IN FRONT BUT OUT OF REACH

If your opponent holds the gun well back out of reach but extends his left arm to frisk you, slap his left elbow with your right hand so as to turn his body to his right.

COUNTER-ATTACK

With your left fist deliver a blow to the base of his skull and quickly step behind him. Reach both hands under his right arm, grasp his gunhand and pull it up into the center of his back into a hammer-lock. Here the disarming takes place. Hit him over the head with the pistol or continue as described in Form #6.

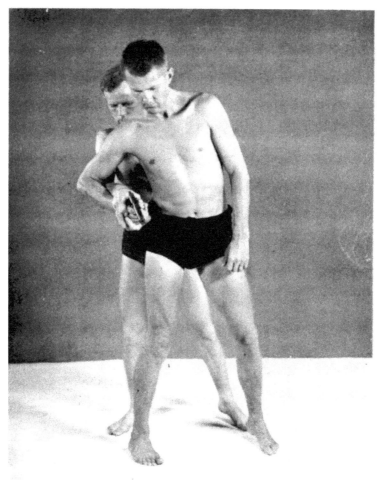

DEFENSE #3

PISTOL HELD IN BACK IN
CENTER OR TO LEFT OF SPINE

Turn to the right bringing your right elbow back and down as you turn so as to strike and divert his gun arm. Hold the upper arm vertical as you turn. Immediately grasp his right hand with your right.

COUNTER-ATTACK

Deliver a blow with your left fist to the base of his skull and perform Form #5.

This is an extremely advantageous position and there are many alternate counter attacks possible:

Throw #3 (if the pistol has been
dropped)
Form #6
Form #7 (possibly)
Form #8 (very good)
Form #14
Escape #12

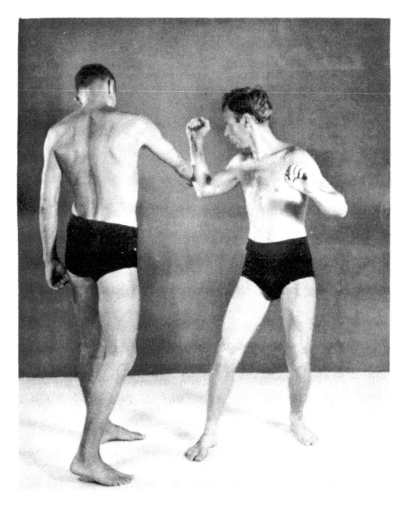

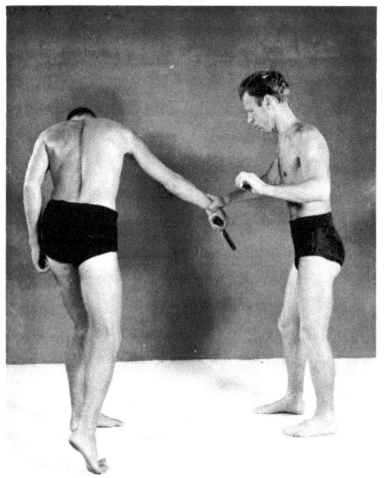

23

DEFENSE #4

PISTOL HELD IN BACK TO RIGHT OF SPINE

Turn to your left bringing your left elbow back and down as you turn so as to strike and divert his gun arm. Hold the upper arm vertical as you turn. Immediately grasp his right hand with your left.

COUNTER-ATTACK

Deliver a right heel of hand blow to his jaw or a fist blow to his throat. With your right knee strike his testicles and then step behind his right leg with your right. Continue as described in Escape #8.

An alternate counter-attack would be to pass your left arm around his gunarm and perform the arm leverage described in Escape #6.

<u>DEFENSE #5</u>

PISTOL HELD VERY LOW IN BACK

Turn right or left as appropriate.
straightening the arm and diverting the gun
with your fore arm.

COUNTER-ATTACK

Same as for Defense #3 and #4.

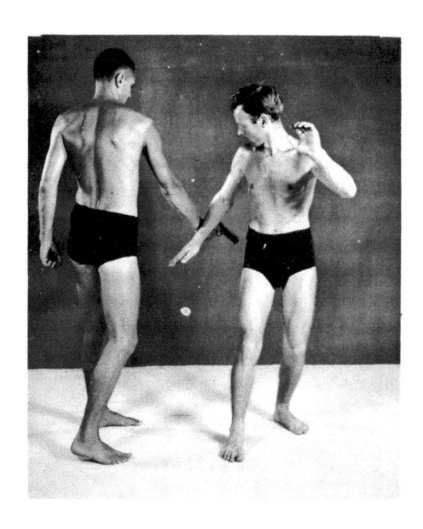

DEFENSE #6

OVERHAND BLOW WITH A CLUB OR KNIFE

Leap in with your right fore-arm held horizontally and stop the blow by letting his descending wrist contact your fore-arm. Instantly slide your right hand down and grasp his right hand.

COUNTER-ATTACK

If you have caught his arm up high before the blow is fully developed use the arm lock described in Form #15.

If the blow is further developed and his arm is lower use Form #7 or the counter-attacks listed in Defense #3 for a pistol held to left of spine.

<u>DEFENSE #7</u>

RIFLE IN FRONT

Your opponent holds his rifle with or without
bayonet at hip level on his right side. His left hand
is extended under the barrel and his right hand grips
at the trigger. Pivot your body to the left so as to
be outside of the line of fire. Slap down with your
right hand at the end o f the barrel to divert the muzzle to his left. Grasp the muzzle with your right hand
fingers on top and thumb underneath.

RIFLE IN BACK

Pivot your body to the right and divert the
end of his rifle to his left with your right arm. Use
the arm as described in pistol defenses, diverting
with upper arm if rifle is high and by straightening
the arm if low. Grasp the muzzle with your right hand,
fingers on top and thumb underneath.

DEFENSE #7
(Continued)

COUNTER-ATTACK

Step in quickly and grasp the butt of the
rifle behind his right hand with your left, fingers
on the bottom, thumb on top. Jerk the rifle toward
you to straighten his arms. Swing your left hand
holding the butt upwards and your right hand holding the muzzle down so as to twist the rifle from
his grasp.

Deliver a knee blow to his testicles with
the right knee, Smash the gun butt into his face
and jump back out of reach, covering him with the
rifle.

An alternate counter-attack would be to
step behind him with your left leg and trip him
backwards over it by pressing against his upper
body as you twist the rifle from his grasp. Use
the rifle butt or bayonet on him as appropriate
when he is down.

DEFENSE #8

UNDERHAND JAB OR SLASH WITH KNIFE

Sidestep and pivot to the left so that you are outside of your opponents arm and his jab passes in front of you. At the same time strike his right wrist with either hand so as to further divert the blow. Instantly grasp his wrist.

COUNTER-ATTACK

If you have caught his hand with your left use the same counter-attacks as in Defense #1.

If you have caught his hand with your right use the same counter-attacks as in Defense #3.

If you have fully perfected Block #3 against kicks so that you can throw yourself down it will provide an excellent defense against a man using a knife in a cautious manner.

DEFENSE #9

BAYONET THRUST

Sidestep and pivot to the left so that you are outside of the bayonet and the thrust passes in front of you. At the same time strike the end of the barrel with either hand so as to further divert the thrust.

COUNTER-ATTACK

Same as Defense #7.

If the opponent is running at you it is well to try to push the end of the barrel down so that the bayonet digs into the ground. This should tear the weapon from his grasp especially if you are then able to grasp toward the butt and lift up on it. The situation here is too variable to detail further counter-attacks. You should be in an advantageous position to gain possession of the weapon or attack him from the rear.

Vital Areas

ATE - MI   "VITAL TOUCHES"

A "Vital Touch" is any blow or pressure that causes
pain, injury or death. Vital Touches are given with the little
finger edge of the hand, the open palm, the heel of the hand,
the stiffened finger, the knuckles, the head, the shoulder, the
elbow, the knee, the heel of the foot and the toes of the foot.
Blows can also be given with a stick or club. Vital touches
are used for two purposes, First: the disabling of an opponent
and Second: as a means of releasing oneself from a disadvan-
tageous hold. On the charts and in this text the lettered spots
are those that fall primarily in the first group and the number-
ed spots those that are used primarily in the second group.

METHODS OF DELIVERING "VITAL TOUCHES"

Edge of Hand. This is a cutting or chopping blow given with the little finger edge of the open hand. Striking area is between the wrist and the base of the little finger. The edge of the hand can be toughened by pounding on hard objects.

Heel of the Hand. This blow is given in the same manner as an uppercut blow in boxing or by driving straight from the shoulder. The hand is held bent back as hard as possible. The heel of the hand can be toughened by pounding on hard objects.

Fist. Fist blows are given with the upper finger joints, the hand being tightly doubled up with the back of it in a line with the upper arm. Fist blows are more effective if some small object is held in the hand such as a small stick or a handkerchief with your loose change tied up in it.

Single Knuckle. Clench the hand letting the knuckle of the middle finger protrude. Press the thumb against the lower joint of this finger to reinforce it. This blow is used for gouging a small area.

Wedge Knuckle. Hold the hand with the upper finger joints in a line with the back of the hand, the lower joints being clenched under.

Straight Finger Jab. Let the two adjoining fingers overlap the middle finger on the inside. Slightly bend all three fingers until the finger tips are at the same level. Use on the solar plexus, armpit and throat.

Front Elbow. Tightly clench the fist and double the lower arm against the upper arm. Hold the elbow up high at the same level as the shoulder. Swing the elbow like a fist.

Back Elbow. Striking area is the back of the elbow. The forearm is held at a ninety degree angle to the upper arm and the hand is held open and rigid.

Front Kick. Deliver with the toe of the shoe. If wearing light canvas shoes or if barefoot kick with the ball of the foot.

Back Kick. Deliver with the bottom of the heel.

Stamping. Stamp with the back rim of the heel.

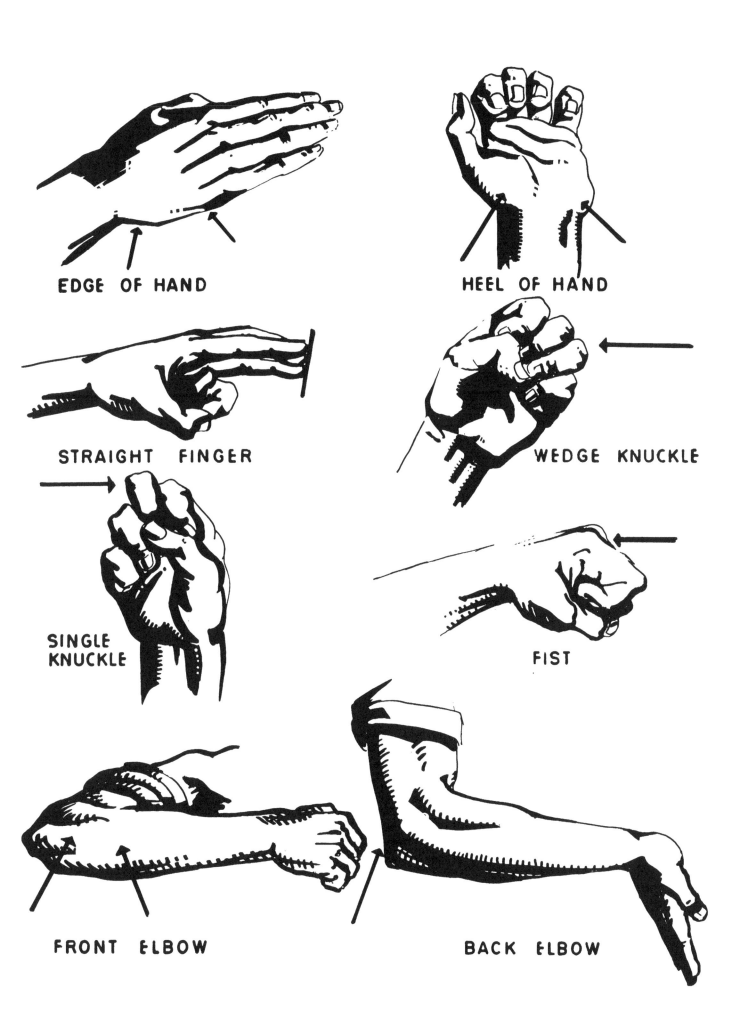

EDGE OF HAND

HEEL OF HAND

STRAIGHT FINGER

WEDGE KNUCKLE

SINGLE KNUCKLE

FIST

FRONT ELBOW

BACK ELBOW

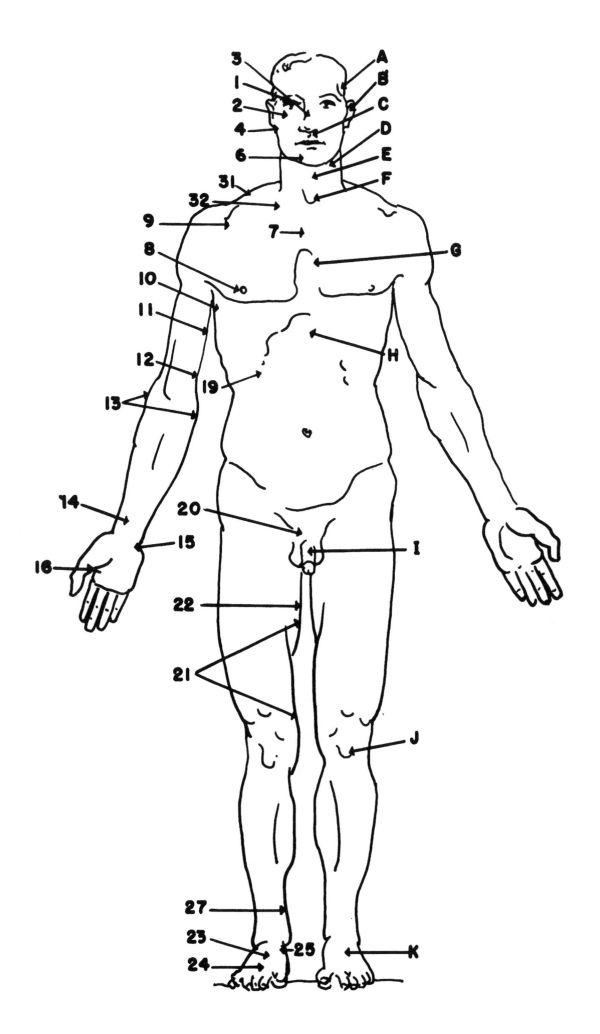

40

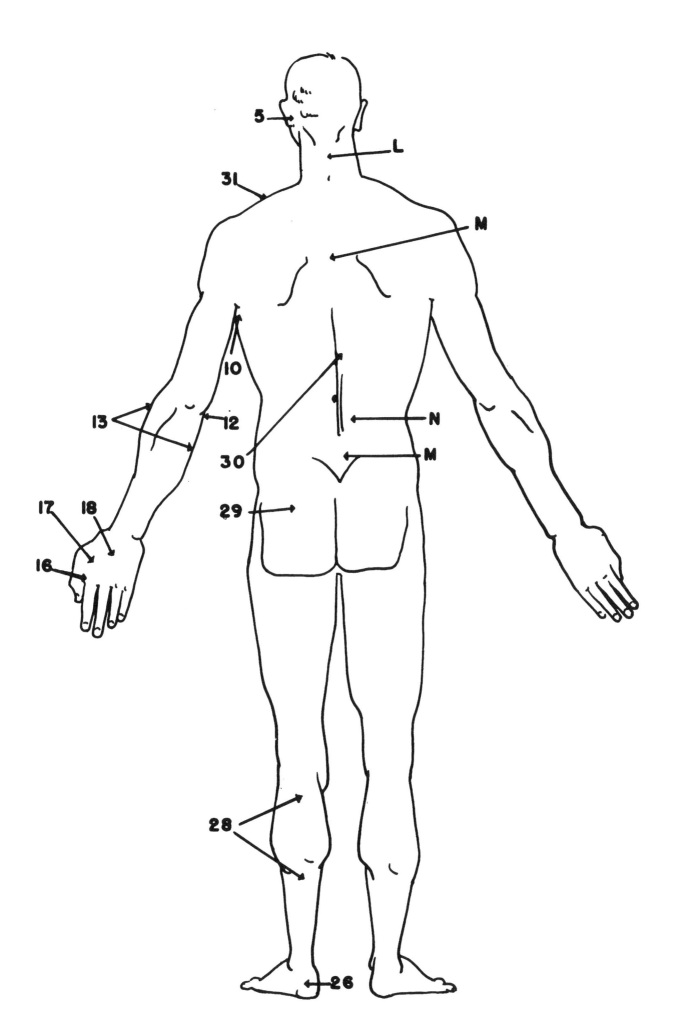

41

A. __Temples.__ Hard blow with the knuckles or point of a stick or club.
Effect: Pain, injury, death.

B. __Ears.__ Concussion blow given with the palms of the slightly cupped hands, delivered to both ears simultaneously.
Effect: Unconsciousness and death.

C. __Upper Lip.__ Edge of hand blow directed up and back directly under the nose close to and against the upper lip.
Effect: Pain, injury, death.

D. __Throat.__ The vagus nerve and carotid arteries run up both sides of the windpipe and are most vulnerable high up under the angle of the jaw bone. An edge of hand blow or pressure as from a choke is used.
Effect: Pain, unconsciousness, death.

E. __Adams Apple.__ Edge of hand blow or pressure directly over the prominence of the adams apple.
Effect: Pain, injury, death. Deforms the larnyx, making speech and breathing difficult or impossible.

F. __Lower Throat.__ Thumb pressure or straight finger jab directly back into the hollow of the throat just under the adams apple and just over the saddle of the breast bone.
Effect: Pain, injury, death.

G. __Heart.__ Heavy crushing blow just to the left of center of the chest with the fist, knee, foot, elbow or club.
Effect: Pain, unconsciousness, death.

H.   <u>Solar Plexus.</u> A deep penetrating blow as from the
       stiffened fingers or the point of a stick just under
       the center bottom of the chest. It is preferable but
       not essential to deliver the blow when the opponent
       exhales.
       Effect: Pain, unconsciousness, and in rare cases,
                death.

I.   <u>Testicles.</u> Any kind of heavy smashing blow or by
       squeezing with the hand.
       Effect: Pain, unconsciousness, death.

J.   <u>Knee Cap.</u> A shattering blow with the toe or heel of
       the shoe or a club.
       Effect: Pain and complete disablement of the leg.

K.   <u>Foot.</u> Stamping with heel or a club on the top arch
       of the foot.
       Effect: Pain and complete disablement of the foot.

L.   <u>Back of Neck.</u> A rabbit punch with the edge of hand
       to the exact center of the back of the neck. This
       must be a slanting downward blow.
       Effect: Unconsciousness, paralysis, death.

M.   <u>Backbone.</u> A heavy smashing blow or kick or a club
       anywhere on the spine especially just at hips level.
       Effect: Unconsciousness, paralysis, death.

N.   <u>Kidneys.</u> Any kind of blow or concentrated pressure
       about an inch and a half each side of the backbone
       and on about the level of the belly button.
       Effect: Pain, injury, unconsciousness.

THE FOLLOWING POINTS ARE ATTACKED
PRIMARILY BY QUICK HARD GOUGES

1. In and up under the frontal bone over the eye.

2. Prominence of the cheek bone.

3. Bridge of the nose. Knuckle or edge of hand blow.

4. Hinge of the jaw bone. Gouge or edge of hand blow.

5. Under the ear in back of the jaw bone.

6. On front bottom of chin in line with dog teeth.

7. Breast Bone.

8. Teats. Pinch and twist.

9. Inside shoulder muscle under collar bone gouging from front against shoulder joint.

10. Armpit. Gouge or straight finger jab.

11. Inside upper arm.

12. Crazy bone. Knuckle blow or gouge.

13. Both sides prominence of forearm muscle. Gouge or edge of hand blow.

14. Wrist where the pulse is taken. Gouge outward (thumb side) against bone.

15. Wrist, end of bone on little finger side of wrist.

16. Pinch muscle between thumb and first finger.

17. High up between thumb and first finger. Pressure against upper bone of first finger.

18. Back center of the hand between the first and second fingers.

19. Straight finger jab or edge of hand blow directed in and up under the lower rib, at sides and sides of front.

20. Along the fold of the groin above the testicles.

21. Along the inner side of the upper leg is a cord that can be gouged from crotch to knee. It is most vulnerable up high on the leg and then again about two inches above the knee and towards the front of the leg.

22. High up on the inside of the upper leg. Slap, pinch, and twist.

23. Arch of the foot, top and a little to the outside.

24. Between the toe bones about an inch above the base of the toes.

25. Half way between the ankle bone and the heel on the inside of the foot.

26. Just under the ankle bone on the outside of the foot.

27. On the inside of the leg above the ankle bone press from back side forward against the shin bone.

28. Prominence of the calf muscle and again about one third of the way up from the bottom of the calf muscle.

29. Going around to the back from the hip bone about four inches and about two inches lower down.

30. Knuckle massage anywhere along the backbone, especially lower down.

31. Prominence of the muscle that runs between the shoulder and the neck. Half way between the shoulder and the neck just to the back of the top. Pressure or edge of hand blow. An edge of hand blow will cramp the head to one side.

32. Close against the side of the neck gouge down in back of the collar bone. This spot is used in resuscitation.

WEAPONS OF OPPORTUNITY

Short Stick. Find a stick about six inches long and about three-quarters of an inch in diameter. Grasp the stick so that it projects about one-half inch beyond the hand on each side. Hit with the ends of the stick. A fist blow delivered while holding the stick will be much more solid than a blow without the stick.

Your opponent will find it difficult to get the stick away from you as it is not long enough for him to grasp. If he grasps your wrist to stop a blow, twist your hand so as to drive the end of the stick into the back of his hand.

Hold the stick with one end in the palm of the hand and the other end projecting out in the same direction and beyond the fingers. Jab into the solar plexus, armpit and throat.

Magazine. Roll a small magazine up tightly and use in the same manner as the short stick.

Sock. Remove a sock and fill it with sand, earth, a small rock or your loose change.

Sand. Scoop up a handful of sand or dry earth and throw it in your opponents eyes.

Cigarettes. Break open several cigarettes and gather the loose tobacco in your hand. Throw this into your opponents eyes.

Beer Bottle. Grasp a beer bottle by the neck and break it over your opponents head. After breaking it jab him in the eyes and throat with the jagged end.

Chair. A light chair held by the back and seat is an effective shield against a man with a knife. Hold it as a shield and jab him with its legs.

Helmet. Throw your steel helmet into your opponents face.

Belt. A heavy belt such as is worn by Marines is helpful in close in fighting. Double it up short and swing the heavy buckle.

Imagination. Use your imagination and you will be able to see other common objects that can be used with deadly effect.

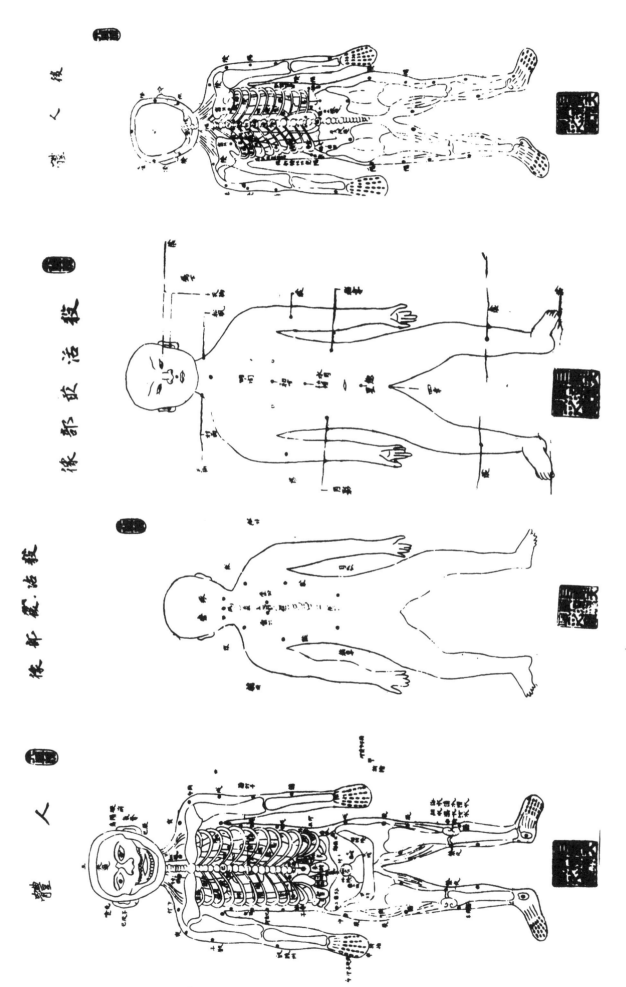

ANCIENT VITAL TOUCH CHARTS OF THE TEN-SHIN-RYU

Kicking

BACK KICK

Your opponent takes a step forward to deliver a blow with his fist.

Take a step backward with your left foot and turn your body sideways to your left.

Lean sideways to your left until your body is horizontal or nearly so. Lift your right leg and double it up, balancing on your left leg.

Deliver a forceful kick to your opponent's kneecap with the bottom of your right heel. This kick will shatter his kneecap.

FRONT KICK

Stand with your right side toward your opponent and raise your right foot up alongside your left knee.

Kick at your opponent so that the toe of your shoe strikes up under his knee-cap.

Kick at your opponents testicles with the arch of your foot.

These are whiplash kicks with your foot returning to it's starting position as fast as it was kicked out.

BLOCK #1 LOW KICK

Your opponent kicks at you. You
have anticipated his kick and see it coming
from the start.

Turn slightly to the left and extend your right leg with the foot turned
sideways. Allow your opponent to strike
his ankle against the hard edge of your
shoe as he kicks.

BLOCK #2 HIGH KICK

Your opponent kicks at you. Sidestep or dodge his kick and grasp his kicking foot from underneath with either or both
of your hands.

Lift his leg until it is horizon-
tal and deliver a kick to his testicles with
the toe of your foot. After kicking him
push his foot up as high as you can above
your head, so that he falls onto the back of
his head.

BLOCK #3 KICKS WHEN ON BACK

You are on your back and your opponent approaches toward your feet to kick you.

Twist up onto your right hip and hook your right foot behind his right ankle from the outside.

Drive the heel of your left foot against his right kneecap. This will shatter his kneecap and knock him down.

From a standing position have your companion extend his right arm, holding it rigid. Grasp his hand with your left, support your weight on it as you drop to your right side and perform the above trick.

Repeat the above taking a short run into it.

Repeat the trick without using your companions supporting arm. Run, throw yourself down and trip.

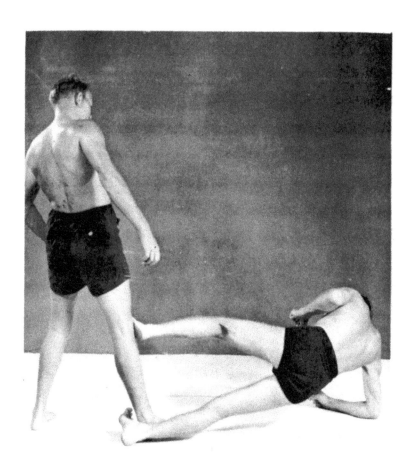

BLOCK #4 KICKS WHEN ON SIDE OR FACE

You are on your hands and knees. Your opponent approaches from your head or side to kick you.

Grasp the back of his heel with your hands and drive your shoulder with force against his knee. Try to hit a little to the side of front on his knee. This will knock your opponent down and will possibly badly strain his knee.

On your back or stomach when your opponent approaches from your side or head, endeavor to grasp his kicking foot and roll your body up onto his leg to knock him down.

Chokes

CHOKES

The carotid arteries and the vagus nerve run up
each side of the wind pipe and are most exposed high up under the angle of the jawbone.

Jiu Jitsu chokes exert pressure on the arteries and
nerves. To a certain extent they choke off the air, but this
is secondary. Pressure on the arteries stops the flow of
blood to the brain. Pressure on the nerve slows the heart
action.

A properly applied Jiu Jitsu choke will render a
man unconscious within ten seconds.

Choking an opponent while standing in front of him
is generally inadvisable as you are wide open to counter-
attack. One front choke is described that is considered
practical because of its extreme severity. The opponent is
rendered unconscious nearly instantaneously and has but little
time for counter-attack.

CHOKE #1

Akenoma "Thumb in the Throat". Grasp the lapels of your opponents coat collar with each hand, your right hand to the left of his neck, your left hand to the right of his neck, your thumbs pointed down and your fingers inside of his collar. The holds should be taken well back, if possible, with only about two inches between the hands at the back of the neck.

Straighten your arms with a jerk as though to pull your hands apart at the back of his neck. Allow your thumbs to be forced into the hollow in the throat just above the breast bone by your effort in straightening your arms.

As a prevention against a kick and to add to this trick, spring off the ground and get a scissors around your opponent's waist. Give a sharp squeeze at the bottom of his ribs as you straighten your arms and quickly regain your feet before he collapses.

64

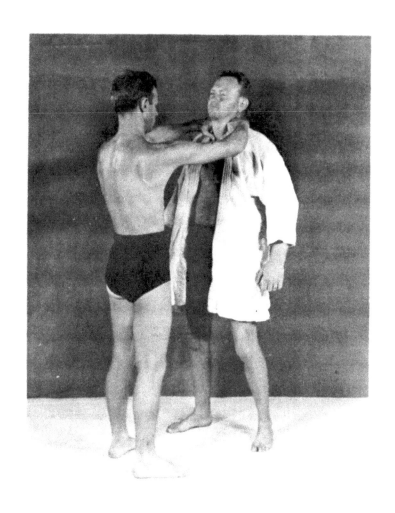

CHOKE #2.

Hikkoshi Keage "Kicking up or
tossing by Drawing Hip". From in front of
your opponent reach around in back of his
neck in such a way that his head is back of
your armpit and his body is in front of you.
Clasp the hand that has this head lock with
the other hand to enforce the pressure or
reach down and grasp his belt in the back.
Place your foot on his abdomen or high on
the inside of his leg, fall backward, kick
upward throwing him on over you retaining
your hold on his neck. Follow him on over
with your own body close to his to come
down with your knees astraddle of him.
With the momentum you have gained from your
double backward somersault jerk up strongly on his head and twist it so as to break
his neck.

This trick is especially applicable
when your opponent rushes you with his head
held low.

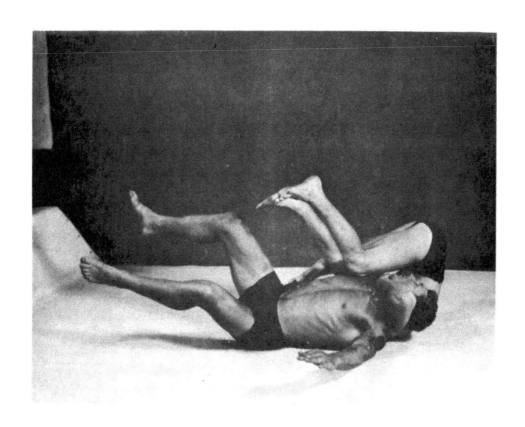

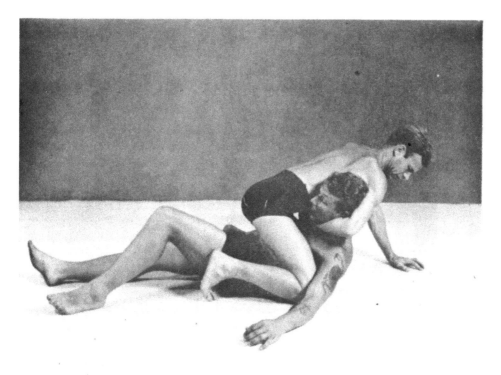

CHOKE #3

Mawari-Iri "Rounding with Lapel".
From in front of your opponent grasp his
left lapel, well back, with your right hand,
thumb inside the collar. Place your left
hand on the back of his right shoulder or
grasp high on his right arm. Push on your
right hand and pull on your left hand so
that you spin him around in front of you.
Your right arm will curl around his throat
and his back will be to you. Pass your
left arm under his left arm and up to the
back of his head. Press with your left
hand and pull with your right to choke him.

After passing your left arm under
his you can reach across his chest and
grasp his right coat lapel instead of
placing your hand on the back of his head.
Pull down on his right coat lapel and back
around on his left coat lapel to choke him.

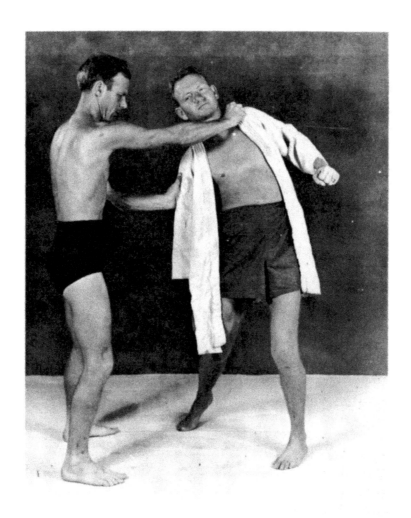

CHOKE #4

Ushiro-Zime "Down Behind".
From behind your opponent, pass your right
arm over his right shoulder, in front of his
throat and under his chin until you can
reach your right hand with your left from
over his left shoulder. Grasp your right
hand so that your left hand is underneath
and the palms together. Bring your left
elbow well down into the middle of his back.
Press your head against his head and exert
the leverage that you have against his
throat. Kick hard against the back of one
of his knees and push so that he will sink
to the ground.

As your opponent goes down drop
to your left knee and place your right knee
in the middle of his back to act as a
counter leverage against your choke.

CHOKE #5.

Hadaka Shime "Strangling Naked".
From behind your opponent pass your left arm
over his left shoulder, in front of his
throat and under his chin. Make sure that
his neck is up snug in the bend of your elbow. Extend your right arm over his right
shoulder. Grasp high up on your right arm
with your left hand. Bend your right arm
and place your right hand on the back of
your opponent's head. Place your forehead
against your right hand. Push with your
hand and forehead so as to force him against
your left arm for the choke.

Kick the back of his knee so as
to force him to the ground and place your
knee in his back for a counter leverage.

KATSU "VIVICATION".

Instructors of Jiu Jitsu are required by the traditions and ethics of the art to teach resusitation to their students at the time that the dangerous chokes and vital touches are taught.

The accepted form of resusitation in this country is the Shaefer Prone method of Artificial Respiration. A system of resusitation that has been used for centuries in conjunction with the practice of Jiu Jitsu is given here. The author has seen this successfully used a number of times.

This is not, however, an accepted form of resusitation by the medical profession of this country. Doctors with whom the author has discussed this have expressed the opinion that they do not see why it should work but that it can do no harm to an unconscious person.

RAIKO "LIGhTENING" KENSEI "RESTORING THE DEAD".

Raise the victim to a sitting position and stand in back of him. Give gentle taps with the knee over the seventh dorsal vertebrae (between the shoulder blades). Press the thumbs deeply into the pectoral arch. This is the hollow space in back of the collarbone which is very pronounced when the shoulders are hunched forward. Practice on yourself to find the spot which is in back of the collarbone close up alongside the neck. When you hit the right spot you will feel sharp pain in your armpit.

The thumb is forced in with a tendency to reach in under the collarbone and the fingers of each hand extend over the chest in front.

Put your mouth close to the victim's ears and shout into his ear.

ARTIFICIAL RESPIRATION COMBINED WITH KATSU.

It is possible to combine the Jiu Jitsu system of mechanical stimulation of nerve centers with the accepted form of resusitation used in this country, the Shaefer Prone method of Artificial Respiration.

Proceed with artificial respiration in the normal manner. When you release the pressure you have exerted to force his exhalation reach up and tap the seventh dorsal vertebrae. Do this without spoiling your timing instantly returning your hands to normal position for the next pressure. After your next release use your time to locate the pectoral arch. Next period gouge into the pectoral arch and shout in his ear. Next period tap the seventh dorsal again. If you have help your companion can apply the nerve stimulus while you concentrate on the artificial respiration.

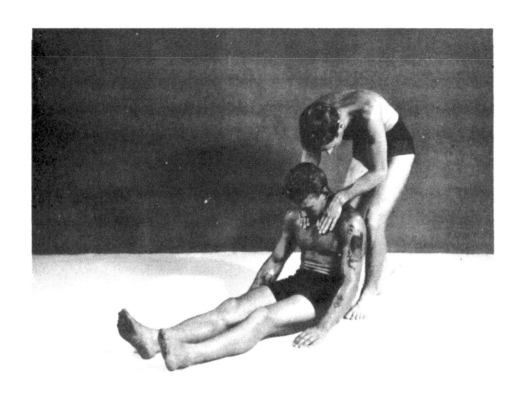

Escapes

ESCAPE #1 - BACK CHOKE.

Your opponent, standing behind you is choking you. He has you bent well backward off balance and has his right forearm against your neck.

Using a wedge knuckle blow strike him on the point of his right elbow with your right hand, endeavoring to hit his crazy bone. After hitting gouge into his crazy bone with your knuckles.

You must be accurate and fast for this break or your opponent will have you unconscious in a matter of seconds.

ESCAPE #2 - GRASPED FROM BEHIND.

Your opponent has grasped you from behind in a bear hug, pinning your arms to your sides.

Reach back and grasp his testicles, pull and squeeze on them.

Stamp down hard with your heel on the arch of his foot.

Swing your head back, driving the back of your head into his face.

If possible to reach up high enough grasp one of his little fingers, bend it back and break it.

Force your arms up to loosen his grasp, give him a back elbow blow to the solar plexus. Grasp his right hand and shoulder and make the throw "Oinage" described in the chapter on rolls and falls.

ESCAPE #3 - GRASPED FROM BEHIND.

Your opponent has grasped you from behind in a bear hug, but on the inside of your arms so that both your arms are free.

Reach back and grasp his testicles, pull and squeeze on them.

Stamp down hard with your heel on the arch of his foot.

Swing your head back, driving the back of your head into his face.

Pry off one of his little fingers, bend it back and break it.

Force your thumb into the point of his elbow on the crazy bone.

Your opponent has his left hand on the top of and clasping his right. Drive the heel of your right hand down onto the thumb side of his left hand, forcing it off.

Your opponent has his right hand on top and is grasping his left forearm. Drive the heel of your right hand down into the knuckles of his left hand so as to bend it and pry it off.

You have broken your opponents grip by one of the above methods and are now holding his left hand with your right with his wrist bent. Clamp his upper left arm under your left armpit and turn around to your left. Press down on his upper arm with your armpit and lift up on his hand as you turn, keeping his arm straight and his wrist well bent. Your opponent will be forced to bend over as you turn. Lift his left hand until it is directly over his left shoulder and bring your left knee with force up into his face.

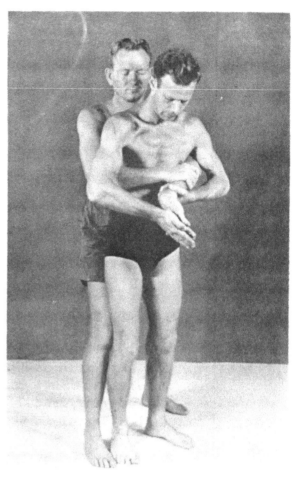

ESCAPE #4 - FRONT CHOKE

Your opponent is choking you from in front, both his hands grasping your neck.

Bring your knee up into his testicles.

Strike him in the armpit with a straight finger jab or a wedge knuckle blow.

Strike him under his lower ribs with an edge of hand blow or a straight finger jab.

Bring the palms of your hands together, swing them up between his arms with force, breaking his grip and forcing his arms apart. Give him a concussion blow over both his ears with the palms of the slightly cupped hands. Butt him in the face with the top of your head.

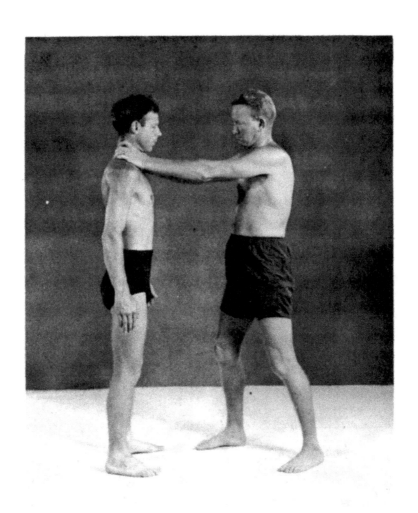

ESCAPE #5 - FRONT CHOKE.

Your opponent is choking you from
in front, both of his hands grasping your
neck.

Grasp the back of his left elbow
with your right hand. Pass your left hand
up inside his arms over the top of his left
arm and grasp his left elbow, reinforcing
the grip you have with your right hand.

Cock your head over to your right
side so as to clamp his left hand between
your head and shoulder against your neck.

Pull strongly on his elbow toward your left and then toward yourself
and down. Your pull should be in such a
manner that it tends to keep his elbow from
bending.

Your opponent will be forced to
bend down as you pull his arm into a vertical position. Bring your knee with force
up into his face.

ESCAPE #6 - FRONT CHOKE.

Force your opponent's arms apart by swinging yours up through them as in Escape #4.

Pass your left arm over the top of his right arm and around it so that your forearm passes under his elbow. Grasp your right arm, high up on the biceps with your left hand. Place your right leg to the outside of his right leg. Press outward against his right shoulder with your right hand and pry upward under his elbow with your left arm. As he falls over your leg and when he has fully lost his balance rear back hard on his arm to break it.

ESCAPE #7 - BEAR HUG

Your opponent, standing in front of you has you in a bear hug, pinning your arms to your sides.

You will have a certain amount of freedom with your lower arms.

Gouge him in the armpits.

Gouge him under his lower ribs.

Grasp and squeeze his testicles.

Gouge into his kidneys.

Knee him in the testicles.

Press down hard with the point of your chin on the top center of the muscle (Trapezius) running between his shoulder and neck.

ESCAPE #8 - GRASPED WRISTS
DIO TE "HAND RELEASE"

Your opponent while standing in front of you has grasped both of your wrists. Break his grip by simply forcing your arms against his thumbs.

After breaking his grip quickly grasp his left wrist and jerk him forward. Place your right leg outside of and behind his right leg and kick it out from under him. At the same time deliver a heel of hand blow to his jaw with your right hand.

As your opponent falls follow him down and drive your right knee into his solar plexus. Hold the grip you have on his right arm, place your left knee high up under his right arm and apply leverage across it to break his arm. With your right hand grasp his windpipe and choke.

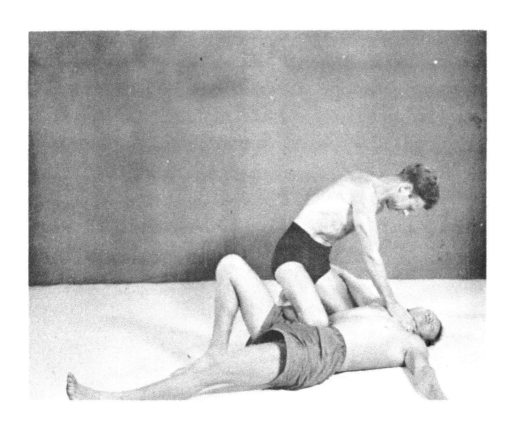

ESCAPE #9 - GRASPED WRISTS.

Your opponent standing in front of you has grasped both of your wrists as they are held up in front of you. Your hands are above his.

Clench your right fist. With the little finger side of your clenched fist strike down hard on his right hand which is holding your left wrist.

This will break his grip on your left wrist and drive his hand down. Open your right hand and continue to press his right hand down and to his left so as to keep it blocked out.

Step in and deliver a blow to the side of his neck with your left elbow. Step back and deliver a blow with your left edge of hand to the front of his throat.

 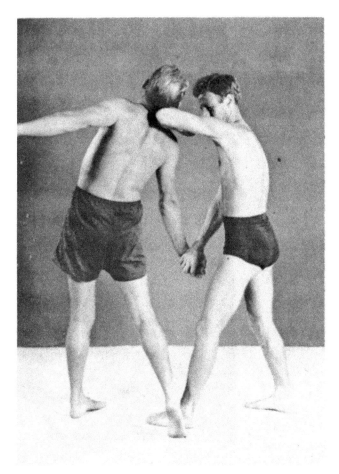

ESCAPE #10 - GRASPED WRISTS.

Your opponent has grasped your right wrist with his left hand. His fingers are on top of your wrist and his thumb is underneath. The thumb side of his hand it toward your hand and the little finger side is toward your elbow.

Hold your right hand extended and stiff and swing your arm so that the forearm approaches a vertical position, the hand higher than the elbow.

Place the thumb side of your stiffened left hand against the little finger side of your stiffened right hand. Using the right hand as a fulcrum and the left as a lever pry his hand off your wrist.

After prying his hand off continue to push it down and to the right with your left hand so as to keep it blocked out.

Step in and deliver a blow to the side of his neck with your right elbow. Step back and deliver a blow with your right edge of hand to the front of his throat.

ESCAPE #11 - GRASPED WRISTS.

Your opponent has grasped your right wrist with his right hand. The thumb side of his hand is toward your elbow and the little finger side is toward your hand. Swing your hand out and up breaking his grasp. Grasp his wrist and pull him strongly forward off balance. Deliver an elbow and edge of hand blow to his neck with your left arm.

 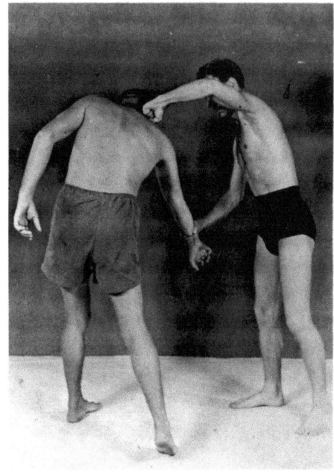

ESCAPE #12 - HAND ON CHEST.

Your opponent has grasped the clothing on your chest with his right hand in order to push or pull you.

Grasp his hand with both of yours as close to your chest as possible, your thumbs underneath and your fingers across the back of his hand.

Turn to your left passing your left elbow over the top of his right arm so that his upper arm is under your armpit. Pull his hand over toward your right side as far as possible when you do this.

Press down on his upper arm with your armpit and pull up on his hand. This will force him down and into position for a backward edge of hand blow with your left hand to his neck.

Do not lean forward when performing this trick. Keep your back straight and prevent his arm from rolling forward.

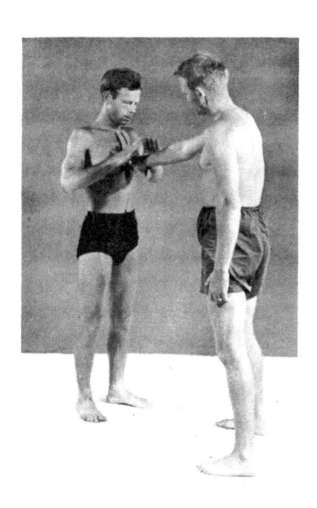 

Combat Forms

YAWARA AND SUTEMI

"GIVING ONESELF UP IN ORDER TO WIN."

The principle of non-resistance used in Jiu Jitsu cannot be stressed too much.

In Jiu Jitsu our strength is never pitted directly against our opponents. Rather, we feint him into applying his effort in a certain direction and then take advantage of him by applying a trick in the direction of his effort. His strength is then helping us to perform the trick instead of hindering us.

We push our opponent backwards, and he resists and pushes against us. We take advantage of his effort by throwing him forward in the direction he is striving to go.

We wish to lift up and pass under our opponent's arm. Pull down on his arm and in resisting us he will endeavor to lift his arm. Quickly change our pulling down effort to a lifting effort and with his help we pass under his arm easily.

WRIST BEND #1.

Your companion raises his hand from his side and holds it so that his finger tips are up and the back of his hand is toward you.

Place the thumbs of both of your hands on the knuckles at the base of his fingers. Place the tips of your fingers at the base of the palm of his hand from each side. Push in with the thumbs and pull back with your finger tips so as to bend his hand onto his wrist.

Here we are working with a lever three or four inches long, the length of the back of the hand. Our thumbs at the base of our opponent's fingers takes advantage of the full length of the lever. If our thumbs are one inch below the base of his fingers we have cut our leverage advantage by 1/4 to 1/3. If we have our own fingers in on top of his wrist it becomes difficult to bend his wrist because our own fingers are in the way. Put only the finger tips at the base of his palm and wing your hands out of the way.

WRIST BEND #2.

Your companion holds his right hand down at his side with the finger tips down and the back of his hand toward you.

Cross your right hand over and place the thumb on his knuckles at the base of his fingers. Place the tips of your fingers at the base of his palm from the little finger side of his hand. Place your left hand in a similiar manner with the finger tips passing around the thumb side of his hand.

This is exactly the same as "Bending a Wrist #1." It is the sides of his hand that have been reversed.

WRIST BEND #3.

Grasp your companion's hand from the side in such a manner that the center of your palm rests across the back of his hand. Your finger tips grip into his palm from the one side and your thumb grips into it from the other. A line drawn from the base of your middle finger to the center of the base of your palm should rest directly across his knuckles at the base of his finger.

Grip hard and bend his hand in on his wrist, his forearm being held or braced in some manner.

WRIST GRASP #1.

Grasp fairly high up on your companion's wrist and you will find that he can still rotate his arm quite freely inside your grip. Grasp your companion's fingers and you will find he can move his arm even more freely.

The correct grip is one in which the heel of your hand just overlaps the heel of his hand. Take this grip and your companion will find it very difficult to rotate his arm.

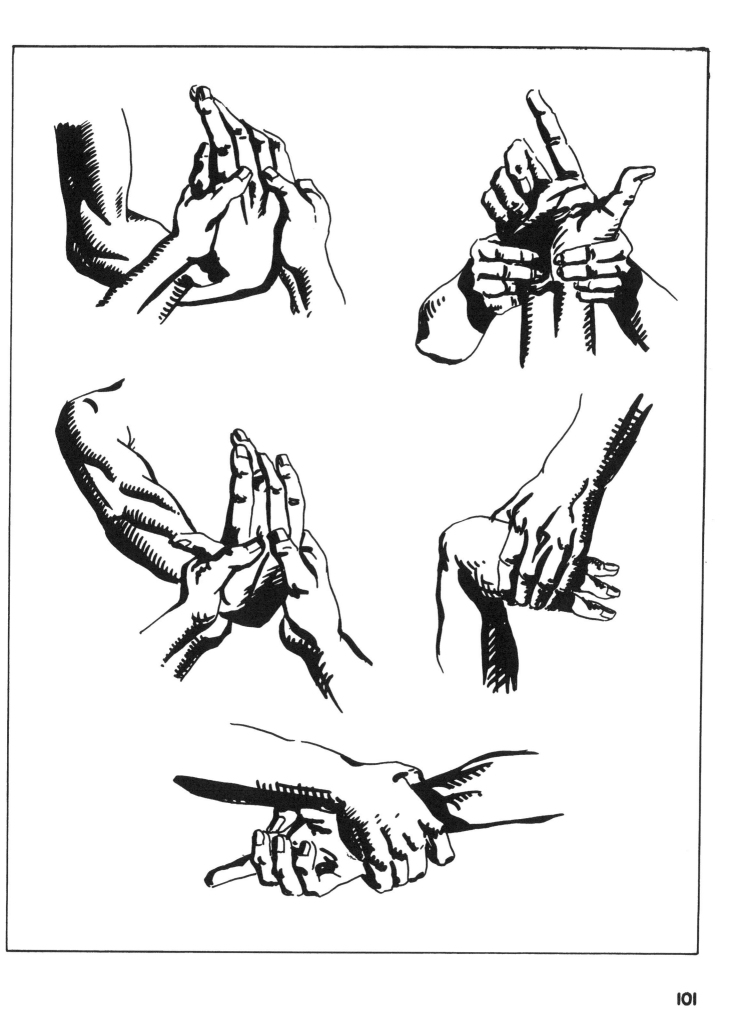

FORM #1 KOTE GAISHI "HAND TURNING".

Grasp your opponent's right hand in "Wrist Bend #1".

Pull back and keep stepping back making every effort to keep his arm straightened out. Bend his hand strongly on his wrist and twist it outward. Place your right foot at the back of your opponent's right knee and he will fall to his back.

When your opponent falls, place his elbow on the ground with his forearm perpendicular. Allow your thumb to slide down his fingers so that the heels of your hands with your full weight come down on his knuckles, breaking his wrist.

After breaking his wrist, kick his temple with your left toe and his lower ribs with your right toe.

FORM #2 KOTE GAISHI "HAND TURNING".

If, when performing Form #1 your opponent manages to bend his arm as you are attempting the outward twist on his wrist, release his hand with your right hand continuing the twist with your left hand. Deliver a blow to his testicles with your right knee and a blow to his neck or jaw with your right elbow. After delivering the blows, continue Form#1 or Form #3.

FORM #3 KATA MAKIKIOMI "SHOULDER WHEEL".

With your left hand take "Wrist Bend #1" on your opponent's right hand. Bend his hand backward toward his shoulder. Pass your right hand under his right upper arm and grasp his right hand in "Wrist Bend #3", letting go with your left hand.

(a) Place your right leg behind his right and twist him down to the ground breaking his wrist and dislocating his shoulder.

(b) While standing, place the point of your left elbow in the bend of his right arm at the elbow where it makes a nest for it to fit into. With your left hand, seize his throat and choke him while you break his wrist with your right hand.

FORM #4 KOTE GAISHI "HAND TURNING".

Grasp your opponent's right hand in "Wrist Bend #2". Bend his wrist strongly and pull back to keep his arm straight.

Your opponent will be forced to turn so that his right side and back are toward you and will bend over.

By carefully swinging his hand up, down, or sideways while you strongly bend his wrist, your opponent can be kept in this position indefinitely or can be made to walk around in this position.

Pull back on your opponent's arm and he will bend down. Kick him in the face with your right foot and he will tend to straighten up, but pull back on his arm and he will lean over so that you can kick him again.

FORM #5 HIKI MAKI UDE "PULLING ARM TWIST".

Grasp the back of your opponent's right hand with your right hand and jerk him strongly forward. Pivot on your right foot, turning your back to him, and placing your left leg in front of him.

Grasp the back of his right elbow with your left hand or grasp his upper arm higher toward his shoulder. Pull back on his hand and push forward on his elbow. He will be forced forward over your leg to his face.

Place your left knee on top of his shoulder joint. Allow your right hand to slip around into "Wrist Bend #3". Grasp his chin from over his neck with your left hand. If his face is turned toward you hit it and he will turn away.

Lift his arm to dislocate his shoulder and bend in on the wrist to break it. As the wrist and shoulder are broken, he will have a tendency to forget about his neck. At this time give a sudden sharp jerk on his chin to break his neck.

This form can also be started by taking his right hand in wrist bend #2 with your right hand.

It is _important_ that when you push him over your leg you _push out_ and _not down_ or he will tend to roll forward out of your hold.

When applying the leverage hold on the ground, his arm should be at right angles to his body.

FORM #6   KOTE GAISHI "HAND TURNING" TENGU "GOBLINS GRIP".

Grasp your opponent's right hand with your right hand in "Wrist Bend #2.". With your left hand, grasp the back of his right elbow and lift up on it. At the same time, bend his wrist and snap his arm around behind him into a hammer-lock.

Reach over your opponent's left shoulder and grasp his chin with your left hand. Force your left elbow down into the center of his back so as to pull his head back. Push into the small of his back with your right hand. Stamp down and forward on the top of the calf of his leg at the back of his knee.

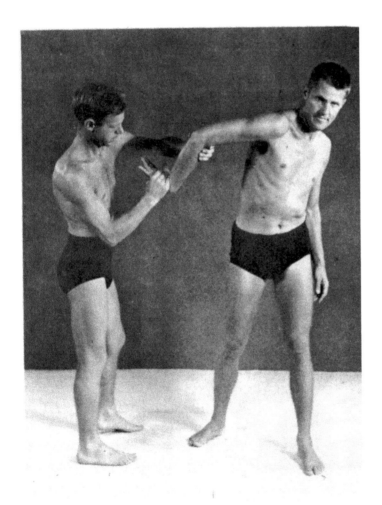 

Your opponent will fall forward on his face. Sit down astride him and force your right knee up under his right arm to hold it. You can now let go with your right hand. Let go with your left hand and dig your fingers sharply into his armpit. Your opponent will pull his left arm back to protect his armpit. Grasp his left arm and pull it up into a hammer-lock. Force your left knee under his left elbow and release your hands.

You can exert considerable pressure on your opponent's arms with your thighs. Both your hands are free to deliver blows to his neck or to grasp his chin and back of his head to break his neck. This is the position used in tying or hog-tying a prisoner.

If, while standing, your opponent tries to strike back at you with his free left hand, release your grasp on his chin and grasp his left arm pulling it into a hammer-lock. Now when your opponent is pushed forward he will not have a free hand to break his fall and will fall on his face with force.

FORM #7. TAKA TE DORI "TAKING ARM UP HIGH".

With your right hand, you have caught your opponent's right hand up high. This position could occur after blocking an overhand blow with a club or knife.

Keep your opponent's arm bent so that the upper and lower arm are at a ninety degree angle.

Grasp his elbow or upper arm with your left hand and push up while you pull down on his right hand. Endeavor to make his elbow pass directly over his hand.

Your opponent will be forced down on his face and you will be in a position to pull his arm up into his back in a hammer-lock. Continue into the "Goblins Grip" described in Form #6.

FORM #8 KATA OTOSHI "SHOULDER DROPPING".

With your right hand, grasp your opponent's right wrist in "Wrist Grasp #1". With your left hand, grasp the back of his wrist reinforcing your grip.

Lift his arm, step in front of him, and pass your left shoulder under his elbow or upper arm from his outside. Bend your knees as you pass your shoulder under his arm. Keep your back straight. Raise up with your shoulder and pull down on his hand to break his arm.

Keep the palm side of your opponent's hand turned up while performing this trick.

FORM #9 KATA OTOSHI "SHOULDER DROPPING".

You are performing the previous
trick Form #8, but your opponent manages to
bend his arm slightly.

Your back is to your opponent.
You have his right arm slightly bent, extended over your left shoulder.

Duck your head under his arm and
place the point of your right shoulder
under his armpit. Pull down and a little
sideways on his bent arm.

By conforming with the principle
of non-resistance, we have now let our
opponent pull himself into a much more
severe leverage than we previously had on
him.

FORM #10   KATA OTOSHI   "SHOULDER DROPPING".

You have started to perform Form #8, but your opponent has managed to bend up his arm before you have ducked your shoulder under it.

Do not resist his effort to bend his arm. Let him bend it, but give a strong outward twist to it. That is, your twist is such that upward pressure is on the little finger side of his hand and downward pressure is on the thumb side.

Place the point of your left shoulder under the point of his right shoulder next to his armpit and pull down on his hand.

Again our opponent's resistance has helped him into a bad leverage.

FORM #11   UDE NO MA   "UNDER THE ARM".

Grasp your opponent's left wrist with your left hand in Wrist Grasp #1. With your right hand, grasp the back of his wrist reinforcing your hold.

Raise your opponent's arm. Place your left foot close to and outside of his left foot. Raise your right foot, turn your back to him, and pivoting on your left foot, step behind your opponent having passed under his arm. Pull his arm into a hammer-lock.

When practicing this trick for speed, keep your companion's hand low as you pass under it. In actual combat, to disable the arm, hold it very high and tight as you pass under it, and pull his hand in high as though trying to put it in the back of his neck instead of the small of his back.

You are wide open to counter-attack and very vulnerable while passing under your opponent's arm during the time your back is turned toward him. It is essential that you pass through this danger area fast. Pull down on your opponent's arm, and in resisting you, he will attempt to raise his arm. Reverse your pulling down effort to a raising effort and, with his help, you pass under his arm rapidly.

FORM #12

While facing your opponent, grasp his left wrist in Wrist Grasp #1.

Raise his arm, and, pivoting on your right foot, turn your back to him, placing your left foot about twelve inches to the outside of his left foot.

With the momentum derived from your rapid turning movement, deliver a blow over his heart with the back of your right elbow.

Maintain the position of your feet and his arm which you have lifted up and held with your left hand. Duck your head under his arm so that it is in front of you. With your right hand, grasp the back of his upper arm.

You are now in position to force him forward over your leg as you did in Form #5.

FORM #13   TAKABASAMI "TAKING HOLD UP HIGH".

Your opponent goes through the motion of striking a blow with his fist straight from the shoulder.

Ward it off with a slight movement of the head to the left, and a light blow or slap to his right elbow with your left hand. Pass your right hand under his extended right arm and grasp his left shoulder as you step in back of him with your right foot. Place your left hand in the small of his back and push him past your right hip. Keep your hold with your right hand. Reach down with your left hand behind you and over his right leg to assist you in throwing him across your hips and bent body.

To throw him, press forward with your right hand and lift behind with your left hand as you bend forward.

Guide your opponent into a sitting position in front of you as you throw him. With your left hand, grasp your right hand palm to palm. Press your knee into the small of his back and your head against his head to choke him.

When you have your opponent balanced before throwing him, it should be evident that by holding onto him and throwing your own body down to the right, you can dash his head on the ground and break his neck.

FORM #14   UDE ORI   "ARM LOCK".

With your right hand, grasp your opponent's right hand in Wrist Grasp #1. Jerk him strongly forward and pass your left arm over the top of and around his right arm so that your forearm passes under his elbow. Grasp your right wrist or place the finger tips of your left hand on your right forearm. Keep a strong outward twist on his hand, that is, upward pressure on his little finger side and downward pressure on his thumb side.

Lift up at your opponent's elbow with your forearm and press down on his hand to break his arm.

Keep your opponent's upper arm clear of his body and avoid clamping it with your armpit agaist your own body.

Throw your hips in for maximum leverage.

FORM #15 UDE ORI "ARM LOCK".

While applying Form #14, your opponent manages to bend his arm at the elbow and is straining up trying to bend it further.

Allow him to bend his arm and, at the same time, turn your body around to the left so that you are facing him. Leave your arms in place relative to each other, that is your left hand is still grasping or touching your right wrist. Relax your grip on his right hand and allow your hand to slide around into Wrist Bend #3.

You will now be facing your opponent and will have a wrist lock on his arm as it is bent up high above his shoulder. Step in back of him with your right leg and force him to the ground with the leverage you have on his wrist and arm.

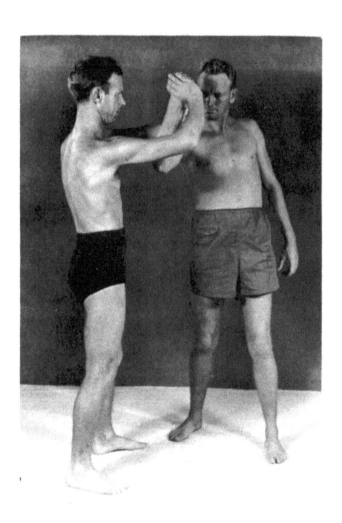 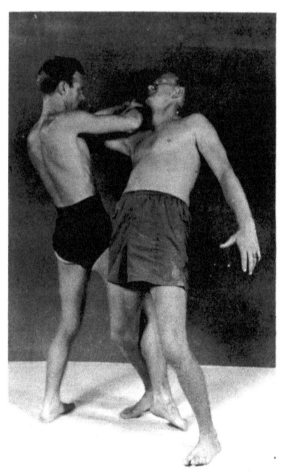

FORM #16 UDE ORI "ARM LOCK".

While applying Form #14, your opponent instead of trying to bend and raise his arm endeavors to turn it against the twist you are applying with your right hand on his right wrist.

Allow him to turn it. Release your grasp on his right wrist and allow your hand to slide into Wrist Bend #3. Bend his arm so that his elbow is braced against your body as you apply the leverage to break his wrist.

 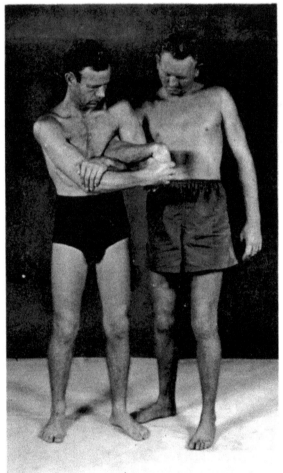

FORM #17

Grasp the back of your opponent's right hand with your left hand, your thumb and fingers encircling his wrist and the heel of your hand resting on the back of his hand. Lift his arm up pulling on it slightly to keep it straight and his wrist will bend. With your right hand, grasp the back of his right elbow and pull it directly under his hand. He will bend down fast and meet your upcoming knee blow with force.

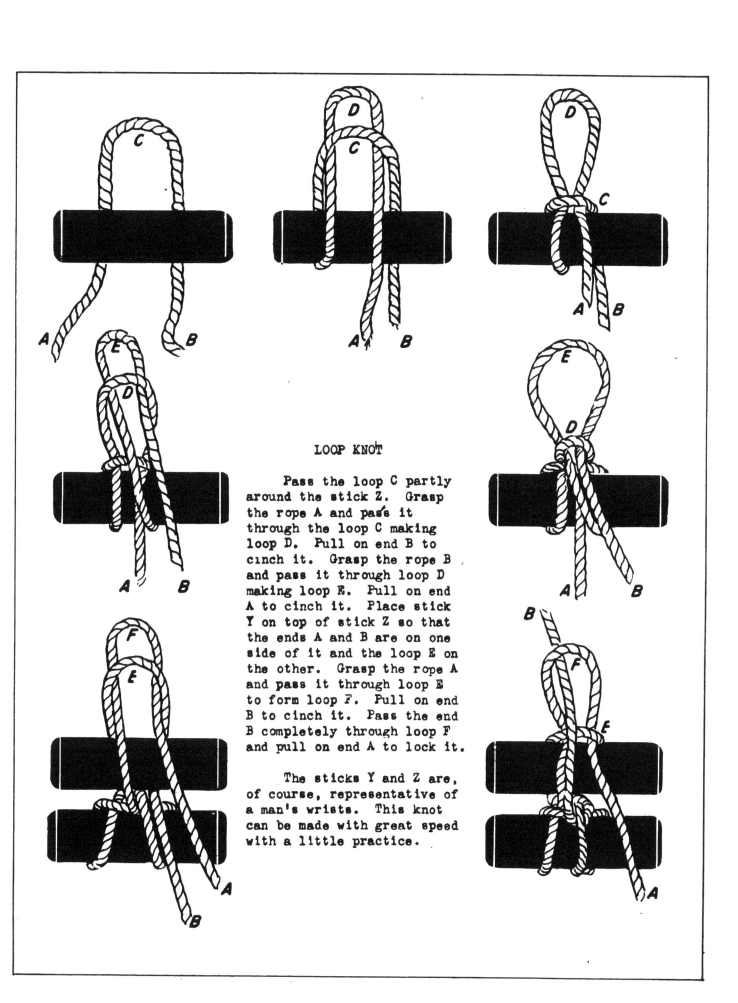

LOOP KNOT

Pass the loop C partly around the stick Z. Grasp the rope A and pass it through the loop C making loop D. Pull on end B to cinch it. Grasp the rope B and pass it through loop D making loop E. Pull on end A to cinch it. Place stick Y on top of stick Z so that the ends A and B are on one side of it and the loop E on the other. Grasp the rope A and pass it through loop E to form loop F. Pull on end B to cinch it. Pass the end B completely through loop F and pull on end A to lock it.

The sticks Y and Z are, of course, representative of a man's wrists. This knot can be made with great speed with a little practice.

TENGU "GOBLINS GRIP".

With your opponent on his stomach, straddle him, facing his head. Hold his arms in a double hammer-lock and force your knees up under his arms. By raising your hips, you will bring pressure to bear on his arms with your upper legs. You can now let go with your hands.

There are many ways of getting your opponent into this position and they are described in other parts of this book.

The advantage of this position is in tying a prisoner. Both your hands are free to do the tying. Your prisoner's hands are in position in front of you to be tied. Your opponent is easily controlled by pressure from your legs against his arms. If he struggles hit him in the face with one of your free hands and bring additional pressure to bear on his arms.

NAWA KAKE "ROPING".

A strong light cord about two fathoms long, is suitable for this work.

With your opponent held in the "Goblins Grip" tie his wrists together with the loop knot using the center portion of your cord. You will now have two long ends left. Pass one end around the front of your prisoner's throat, and back under his tied wrists. Draw up on it so that his arms are pulled up and his head back, adjusting the pressure so that he is not choked unless he struggles. Secure the end of it. You can now help your prisoner to his feet and lead him away with your second long end. If you wish to leave your prisoner, pull up one of his legs and take a round turn and half hitches around his ankle with your second long end.

127

Club Fighting

HOLDING A STICK OR LIGHT CLUB.

As an aid in describing these tricks we will call one end of our stick the handle and the other end the point.

Practice giving the stick a short flip from one grasp and catching it in an alternate grasp.

Grasp #1.

With your right hand, knuckle side up, grasp the stick so that the point and about one fourth of the stick extends out from the little finger side of your hand and the handle with the greater length extends out from the thumb side of your hand.

Grasp #2.

Hold the stick in grasp #1 with your right hand, knuckle side up. With your left hand palm side up grasp about one fourth of the way from the handle end.

Grasp #3.

With your right hand knuckle side up grasp the stick so that the handle and about one fourth of the stick extends out from the thumb side of your hand and the point with the greater length extends out from the little finger side of your hand.

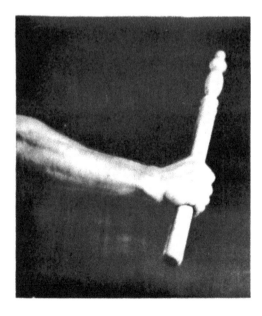 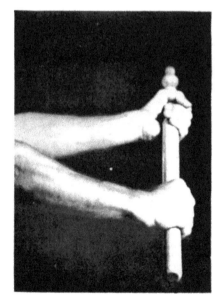

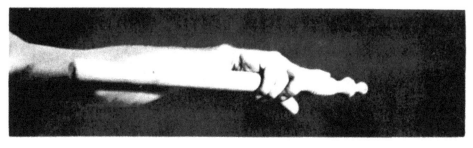

STICK HELD IN GRASP #1.

Swing the handle end up over your left shoulder. Spring in lash down to strike your opponent's shins and spring out again.

Swing the handle end up over your left shoulder. Spring in and strike at your opponent's neck and side of his head with the handle end.

Swing the handle end up over your left shoulder. Swing it as though you were going to strike his head with the handle end. Instead jab him with the point in the eyes, temple or throat.

As you swing your opponent attempts to block your blow by grasping your right wrist. Pass the point end of the stick over his wrist. Pass your left hand under your right arm and grasp the point, the knuckles of your hand being up. You now have a powerful leverage on your opponent's wrist. Swing both hands down hard to break his wrist and pull him forward off balance. Raise the stick and strike him across the back of the neck with the handle end.

From behind your opponent pass the handle end of the stick from his right side across in front of his throat. Hit him hard on the right side of his neck with your thumb as you do so. Pass your left hand over his left shoulder, palm side up and grasp the handle end of the stick in Grasp #2. Force the elbow of your left arm down into the center of his back and press the top of your head against the back of his head to choke him.

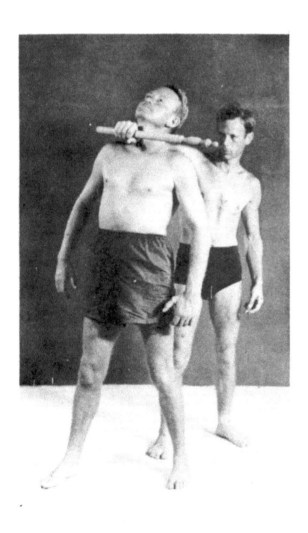

STICK HELD IN GRASP #2.

Hold the stick horizontal in front of you and use it as a block against the opponent's knife or club.

With the club held horizontal the center of it can be thrust into the opponent's throat or smashed down on his face.

Hold the stick with the left hand above and forward of the right hand. Thrust up under the opponent's chin or solar plexus with the handle end.

Swing the handle end up over your left shoulder and jab with the point into his face or throat.

STICK HELD IN GRASP #3.

Allow the point end to rest along the right forearm. Hold the forearm horizontal and use as a block against the opponent's knife or club.

Thrust into the opponent's throat, face, and solar plexus with the handle.

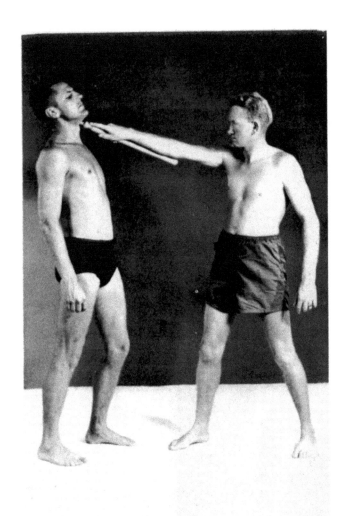 

From behind your opponent pass the point end of the stick from his left side across in front of his throat. Hit him hard on the left side of his throat with the little finger side of your right hand as you do so. Pass your left arm under your right arm, over his right shoulder and grasp the point of the stick with the left hand palm side up. Force the elbows apart to choke him. Holding your grasp on the stick turn to your right so that your back is to your opponent. Keep your back straight and bend your knees so that your hips are low. Suddenly straighten your legs and bend forward to break his neck.

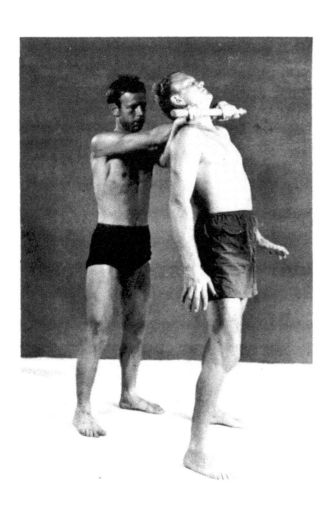

Sentry Stalking

Sentry Stalking combines Scouting and Hand to Hand Combat.

This chapter will treat with the Hand to Hand Combat phase.

Review your lessons on scouting. Absolute stealth and thorough preparation are essential. Eliminate all noisy equipment. Camouflage yourself properly. Take cognizance of sun and shadows. Take advantage of cover. Study the sentries every movement carefully before attacking.

It is claimed that human beings instinctively feel the close presence of another person. Take no chance on this. When close enough spring the remaining distance.

ATTACK #1. HATCHET

When attacking with a hatchet, your aim is to cut the spinal column with one stroke. The neck is the primary target. If the neck is well protected with the helmet or other equipment, attack the spine at about kidney level.

ATTACK #2. KNIFE

Hold the knife in the right hand. Spring on the sentry, land-
ing with a knee in the small of his back. Slap the left hand over his
mouth and pull his head back and to the left. Sever the juglar vein and
wind-pipe with the knife.

ATTACK #3. CLUB

Review the methods of choking with a club in the chapter on Club Fighting.

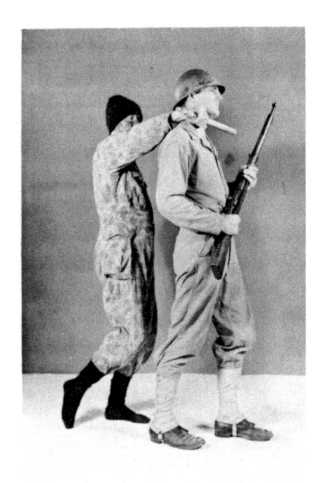 

ATTACK #4. PIANO WIRE

A loop of piano wire is held with the hands crossed. Place over the sentry's head, around his throat, and jerk tight.

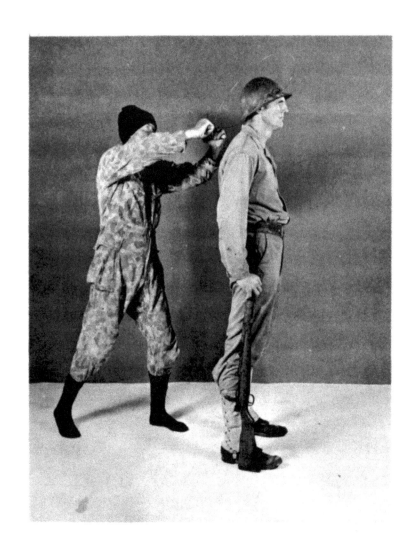

ATTACK #5.   BARE HANDED ONE MAN

Perform Choke #4 "Ushiro Zime" or
Choke #5 "Hadaka Shime", giving a sharp
blow against his wind-pipe with the arm that
is passed in front of his throat and a hard
knee butt against the base of his spine.

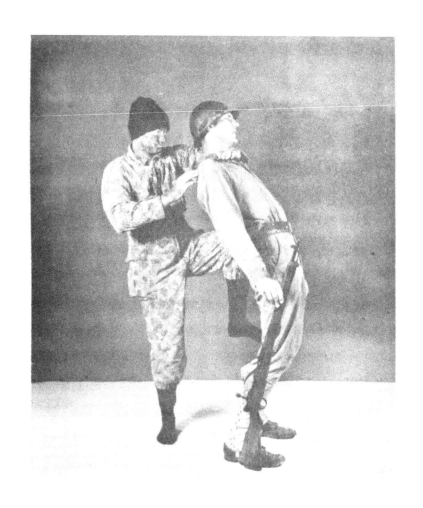

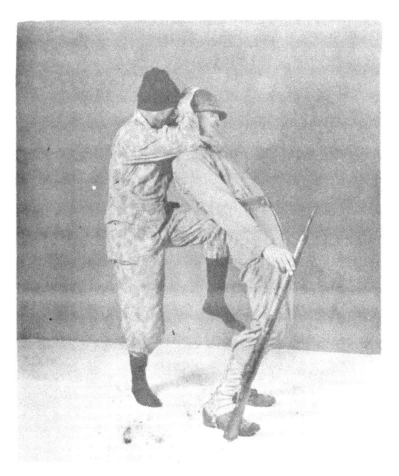

ATTACK #6.   TWO MEN

Two stalkers can work against one sentry with one hitting him high and the other hitting him low around the knees.

The man hitting high should hit just a fraction of a second before his partner and thrust his hand instantly over the sentry's mouth to prevent out-cry.

The low man will maintain his grip around the sentry's knees while the high man chokes him or cuts his throat.

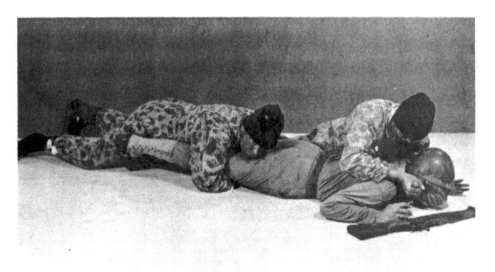

Knife Fighting

THE USE OF THE KNIFE IN CLOSE COMBAT

The knife is one of man's oldest known weapons of combat. Continual improvement in the range of weapons from the spear to the bullet propelling gun, has placed the knife in the category of a secondary weapon of combat, to be used in emergencies only. There are many advantages to this secondary weapon. First, a knife has many uses other than combat, and is one of the most valuable pieces of equipment for a man away from civilization. Second, the knife is a noiseless weapon, and as such, is extremely valuable in sentry stalking and silencing individual enemy outposts and isolated sentries. The knife is light and easy to carry, making it a valuable weapon to fall back upon in event of an emergency. It has a decided moral factor in intimidating an enemy not trained in its use. It must be borne in mind, however, that the knife is a weapon that calls for close-in combat, and that along with developing a proficiency in handling it, a realization of its limitations, since no person, however well trained he may be with a knife, can hope to successfully attack an enemy armed with a gun who is aware of the presence and location of the attacker.

Just as all weapons must be chosen for their efficiency, so must the combat knife. The type knife best suited for close combat is a well balanced, double edged weapon. In this case, balance does not refer to the necessary balance for throwing, but rather for easy handling. Very few people carry more than one knife with them in combat, and to consider throwing that knife away at an opponent instead of holding it for future use, might be considered foolhardy by the majority. The blade, in addition to being double-edged, should be from six to eight inches in length, as a blade shorter than six inches may not be able to reach certain vital areas, and one longer than eight inches becomes cumbersome and awkward. It should be not more than an inch in width at the widest part, and should taper to a sharp point. The haft of the weapon must be of sufficient length to be touched by all the fingers and rest against the heel of the palm of the hand, with a guard of sufficient size to act as a possible deflector for an enemy blade and to prevent the owner's hand from slipping down onto the blade if a bone should be encountered in the thrust. Above all, the blade should be of good material that will not bend permanently or snap if a bone is encountered.

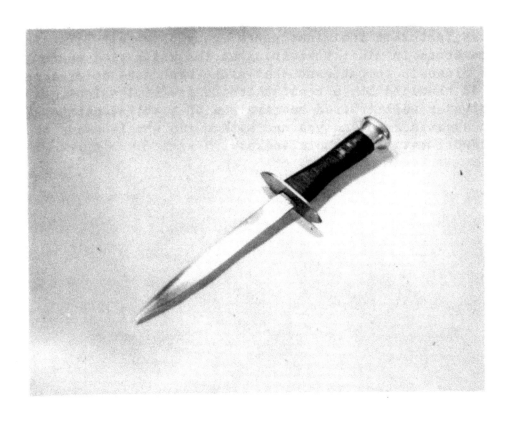

Needless to say, this weapon must be cared for properly at all times, since the difference between a keen knife and a dull one may be the difference between life and death to the owner. A dull knife is only a hindrance and useless weight. Keep the blade well honed and sharpened. If at all possible carry a small hone with you, perhaps even in a compartment of the knife scabbard, and use it whenever the need occurs. On many occasions there will be the temptation to thrust a knife into a fire, perhaps with a bit of food for cooking, perhaps for sterilization. Heat takes the temper from a blade in short order. Do not use this knife as a cooking implement or as a medical instrument except in the most dire emergency.

In combat the knife should be held with the blade flat and parallel to the ground, point toward your opponent's midsection. The hand should clasp the hilt, knuckles towards the ground, with a firm pressure exerted by the thumb and first two fingers. The little finger and ring finger should rest lightly against the upper part of the hilt, holding it against the heel of the palm and movements of the blade should be effected by tightening and loosening these fingers.

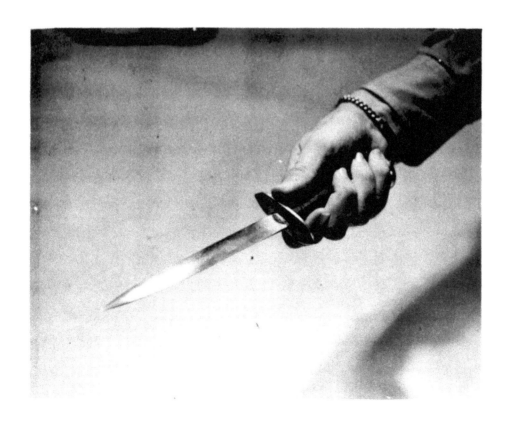

The proper stance for close combat with the knife is one facing the opponent directly with the feet apart sufficiently for good balance, weight equally distributed but thrown forward mostly on the balls of the feet to allow quick movement in any direction. Knees should be slightly bent and the upper part of the body inclined towards the opponent. Upper arms should be close to the sides of the body, but not rigid, with forearms parallel to the ground hands extended toward the enemy, one holding the knife, the other as a guard and an aid to you in combat.

If there is sufficient warning to you and your opponent is also armed with a knife, it is advisable to wrap a coat or other material around the forearm of the guard arm, as this may be useful in warding off an opponent's thrust.

GENERAL COMBAT SUGGESTIONS

       In combat against an unarmed man or one armed with a knife or club, hold your knife in such a manner that the point is always toward your opponent. Your movements should be accomplished with a quick stepping motion such as used in boxing, remembering to maintain balance at all times and to avoid crossing your legs in such a way as to make movement in any direction impossible. Keep the knife weaving slightly from side to side and discourage any attempts of the person opposing you to close with you by short slashes at his hand and arms as they approach you.

       Your guard hand must be available at all times to block thrusts or blows and to attempt to pull or push your opponent off balance, this of course to be followed by a knife attack on your part.

       If the opponent makes a thrust or aims a blow toward you, avoid it by side-stepping, and, using your guard hand as a grasping hand, (see illustration) follow through with your knife.

Whenever possible it is better to cut than stab, as a cut will sever a vein or artery and leave your knife free, while a stab may miss any vital area and the knife may stick momentarily. If a stab is indicated by the position into which you have drawn your opponent make your withdrawal a cut toward the body surface.

The following chart is an indication of areas of the body vulnerable to a cut. This is not to be accepted as the only place to use your knife, since a cut anyplace upon the body aids in demoralizing your opponent.

In this type of close combat, bear in mind all of the defences against a knife that have been brought forth in other chapters of this manual, and guard against this. It is possible that your opponent has had the same type instruction as yourself.

A man with a knife is particularly vulnerable to sand, tobacco, pepper and other irritants thrown in the face or eyes. Guard against your opponents taking advantage of this. It is well also to remember that a little foreign substance in your opponent's eyes may tip the balance of the scales of victory toward you.

It is recommended that all personnel practice knife fighting against one another using dummy knives or taped blades until they have become proficient in taking advantage of their opponent's errors of balance or guard. Knife fighting is not similar to fencing, in which there are recognized engagements, parries and thrusts. It should be regarded as a combination of Jiu Jitsu blocks followed by the knife to your opponent's vital areas.

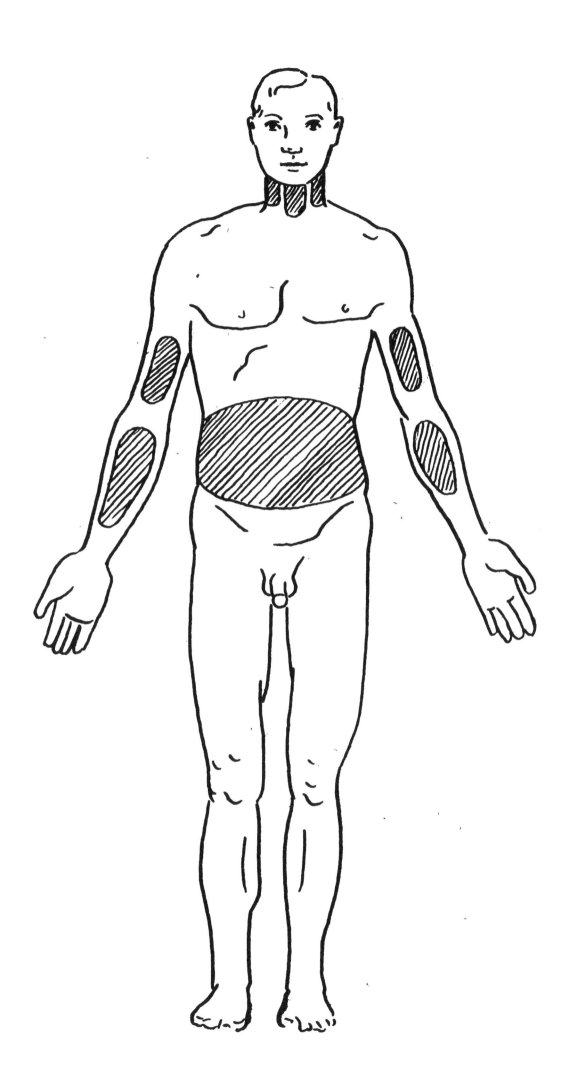

PREPARED
BY THE
TRAINING AIDS OFFICE
FOR
AMPHIBIOUS SCOUTS

OFFICIAL U S NAVY
PHOTOGRAPHS
BY
PHOTOGRAPHIC LABORATORY

U S N A T B
FT. PIERCE   FLORIDA

1 AUGUST 1945

LITHOGRAPHED BY
JANET
PUBLICATIONS SECTION

Lightning Source UK Ltd.
Milton Keynes UK
UKHW051102281022
411251UK00012B/680